I0605492

Ithaca

Ithaca

POEMS

David Lehman

WINNER OF THE NEW CRITERION POETRY PRIZE

First American edition published in 2026 by Criterion Books, an imprint of Encounter Books, an activity of Encounter for Culture and Education, Inc., a nonprofit, tax-exempt corporation.

www.newcriterion.com/poetryprize
www.encounterbooks.com

Manufactured in the United States and printed on acid-free paper. The paper used in this publication meets the minimum requirements of ANSI/NISO Z39.48–1992 (R 1997) (Permanence of Paper).

Library of Congress Cataloging-in-Publication Data Is Available

Information for this title can be found at the Library of Congress website under ISBN 978-1-64177-511-3.

Contents

Ithaca 1

Gifts Reserved for Age 37

"Now that he was here . . ." 41

Leap of Faith 42

Dream Audience 43

The Triumph of Bullshit 44

Doing Philosophy 45

Think About It 46

Que sais-je? 47

Masks of Woe 48

The Trial 49

Good News 50

Breakdown 51

Creation 52

Love and Destiny 53

September Evening 54

The Only Real Thing 55

Senior Seminar 56

Where He Felt Free 57

Grand Central 58

The Commuter 59

May Day 60
"Criticism is death" 61
A Red Mercedes 62
Utopia (No Place) 63
A Working Heaven 64
Lazy Days 65
The Eternal Moment 66
Lessons Learned 67
History 68
The Pious Donors 69
"Not that he was here . . ." 70

Acknowledgments

Thanks to Dana Gioia, Ron Horning, Mary Jo Salter, Rachel Hadas, Glen Hartley, Stacey Lehman, and Mary Jo Bang for reading this manuscript at various stages and making suggestions. Thank you to Paula Deitz of *The Hudson Review* for publishing fifteen of these poems and Ryan Wilson for publishing one of them in *Literary Matters*. I'm grateful, too, to Robert Erickson, who shepherded this work from manuscript to finished book with exemplary skill and attention to detail.

for Mary Jo Salter

Ithaca

I.
Ithaca

Hereux qui, comme Ulysse, a fait un beau voyage.

—Joachim du Bellay

1.

Happy as Ulysses is he who ventures forth,
who leaves behind his idols and his homeland
and mourns the loss of his mariners
shamed like hogs under a witch's spell
or swallowed whole by a one-eyed colossus and yet
he opposes the wind with his beard of sea salt
after one more failure clinging to a spar.
And the poor cottage of an October oracle,
with leaves burning in the distance of a miracle,
absent the flames and amber lights eternal,
is as dear to him as the hospital bed he left
on the appointed day, walking the whole way,
quickening his stride as if he were sprinting
like a sandaled youth past the lotus-tempted sailors.

2.

What did he believe in? God—or nothing,
which didn't amount to the same thing.
There was love, and there was lovemaking,
the stuff of collegiate heartbreak morphed
into a porn classic by a French libertine
writing under the pen name Tiresias
still thirsty for sacrificial blood in Hades
quizzed by nobody special going to Ithaca.
What he wants is to return to the fork
in the road forty years ago. What he gets
are directions: "You can't miss it."
In a soundproof room, walled with cork,
he hears the song, has no regrets.
If he sees her face he will kiss it.

3.

What did he believe in? He thought about it,
puffed on his pipe, emptied the ashes,
refilled the bowl, lit it, puffed again,
said "yeah," and blew out the match.
But then he puffed some more and
refused to choose between death as
oblivion on the one hand and immortality
on the other, and furthermore doesn't
the immortal as opposed to the permanent
exist as merely a poem: a lovely, glorious nothing
that a young man crafted at three
in the morning to woo a young woman
whose name he cannot recall now that
sixty winters are on his head and hers?

4.

What did he believe in? Marriage, she said,
changing the subject. He carried the ladder
painted the hall changed the oil in his truck
fixed the leak, wiped his brow, sipped
tea with rum and lemon juice, and napped
with the light on, a book open on his lap,
as the day waned and his wife prepared
a special dish for him, though he is nothing
more than a functionary, a low-level diplomat
negotiating the next war. One is always
on the way. The man walks home
from work, a familiar mile of drug stores
and butchers, and then, quickening,
he sees the lights on in the top-story flat.

5.

Happy the man who voyages in the vanguard
with crazed mariners, reluctant prophets,
compulsive liars, and tale-tellers, as the flask
of brandy is passed from hand to hand
and the tobacco smoke fills the air like an arena
in a black-and-white movie about brawlers
from the Bronx and guys who fixed the fights.
Happy the worker on Friday nights
and the woman singing of her sorrow
and her lust for Ulysses tied to the mast
who hears the longing that matches his own.
What does he believe in? Yesterday,
but a yesterday that has not yet come to pass
or to grief, like his naive belief in the gods at play.

6.

What does he believe in? God.
The torturer smiled. God? Which god?
The god who argued with Abraham,
who tempted Abraham and spared Isaac,
who wrestled with Jacob and gave Joseph
the power to interpret dreams? Or the god
who blessed the meek forsaken by his father?
He smiled sadistically. Enjoy your cigarette
and your shot of scotch, he said. You believe
in lucid days and ludic nights,
in words, wine talons, water-lights,
the fog in the fir trees.
You will know death to the bone—
the climate of the grave.

7.

What does he believe in? He believes
envy is to the present as hypocrisy was to
fashionable Parisians in 1855. He believes
we are better off in calculable ways yet
guilt remains the constant in the equation
and nothing reeks of meaning like Crusoe's
unused knife on the dresser. His collections
amuse him yet days go by without them.
But shelves he cannot pass without staring
at the spines of the books he read in college
and can still recite their openings (*The Trial*,
The Good Soldier, *The Birth of Tragedy*) and
endings: the happy major's "Hot dog!"
the kids shouting "Hurrah for Karamazov!"

8.

Happy the hero who, like Ulysses,
heeds the voice of the reckless sea
and survives the loss of his crew because
the gray-eyed goddess of wisdom
sees herself in his eyes. Happy the man
who heard what no other mortal heard
and saw what others have only
dreamed they have seen. Happy
the athlete in the sunlight though he
will die young and the chapter will end
with the man who gets on the bus and
believes that at the end of the journey
he will reach home in time for the toasts
to his absence and his rivals' empty boasts.

9.

What did he believe in? Biology,
anatomy, and the destiny of all creation
which admits of no exception
to the slow decay of time
or the rapid route to the underground,
in the dead vast and middle of the night
with no pain or with a surfeit of fright.
Happy the hero who worries less
about his mistress's unholy mattress.
Happy as Ulysses on completing
his journey in Ithaca is he upon repeating
a lifetime of fake cheer and cheating
in an office building on Park Place,
an easy walk from the A train.

10.

Each sunset stayed for its allotted time.
The darkness came on as if someone threw a switch.
What did he believe in? The darkness.
But was there anything behind or beyond it?
The question bothered him, but the hours he spent
in the fifth-floor conference room had taught him
to suspend the discussion while sitting on committees
charged with judging the work of other committees
or in mindless crowds cheering for the underdog
in a game whose rules he barely understands
or chatting up the woman in the gray pencil skirt
at the gallery opening of the sunset show
with a Y-shaped glass full of her orange scent
and the afterglow of gin chilled to bone zero.

II.

What did he believe in? The death of God
announced by a syphilitic madman
on the radio for servicemen abroad
at halftime after the benedictions and anthems.
It was futile but could no more be resisted
than an old man's wish to be young, but she
interrupted his reverie. What about me?
All right, he said, accepting the tea, the jam,
the toast, the lemon, and the bowl of sugar.
I'll bite. What do you believe in? She ate
a biscuit before answering. In you, of course.
You're the only thing I believe in. You're
a beautiful liar, he smiled. But I love thee,
and when I love thee not, chaos is come again.

12.

Happy the man who cultivates the illusion
that he believes in nothing
but the curative powers of the summer sun
and the pleasures of the mind
as he contemplates performing one last work
of noble action before the ban on books begins.
Happy the fellow who walks the city streets,
infiltrates the crowd, leaves messages for
strangers to read later, runs on anxiety,
a cloud of unknowing protecting him.
He knows what to do if someone shouts fire.
The go-go ego prohibits lamentation
for object loss in childhood, fear of castration
in the phallic period, dread of the superego's ire.

13.

What does he believe in?
He believes in lateness.
He arrived late last night.
He came to his senses too late
to recover anything or rescue anyone
from the burning house.
He watched it burn from the road.
He believes that a genius lived here
in a room exactly like his
with a window overlooking
an array of pines some deer and a lake
with some lights twinkling on the rocks,
and he is writing these words
in this room in the burning house.

14.

The mariner sat on the barstool sipping a beer.
He believed in two things: the Yankees this year,
and J. P. Morgan–preferred, two thousand shares,
a handsome profit for the risk-on buccaneer.

The clever vixen with the crimson veneer
beside him orders a Brandy Alexander
and laughs at herself, because she "ordered
a 'girl drink,'" she says. "An X-rated milkshake."

Was it for this that they came, this break
in the routine, the waves perpetual, a sudden surge
in a changeless ocean, where the sun blanks the brain

and darkens the skin, and in their cabin,
in the shade between two palm trees, they merge
their midday bodies and sleep it off like a sin?

15.

What was he selling? Confidence,
always in short supply. What did
he believe in? That he would make the sale
get the girl make his mark seal the deal
and lie in bed smoking in the morning
while she put on her makeup in the mirror.
The memory made him wince if only because
the girl wasn't supposed to be killed.
It was a long time ago and few witnesses remained.
They could have come up with a better cover story.
Car crash, her in the passenger seat,
while he and his pals in Paris and Rome
went whoring and drinking and bumming meals
in the two years missing from his résumé.

16.

Happy the man who resists
the panic of change
who abandons the metropolis
smuggles ideas, spies on the goddess,
sneaks into her fortress,
and takes up residence within.
On her island they play
calypso music all day
and all day he sleeps
and she sleeps and he never asks
what she believes in and
she never asks for his opinion
and at night when the beach is empty
they swim naked in the sea.

18.

Happy the man who asks not judges not,
empties his pockets ungrudgingly,
protests what he is powerless to prevent,
and eats and drinks despite the death
of a parent or a princely child. Happy the sons
and their sisters seeking happiness
without knowing what it is, and that is
what they believe in, the pursuit
of something lying ahead of them
like a faint orange glow behind a distant bluff
warning the sailors of rough waters ahead
until one of them, praising the Lord,
leaps overboard,
and calm returns to the sea.

17.

What did he believe in? Not nature,
indifferent to him, nor history,
indifferent to morality, but the delirium
of a galley slave with a Roman overseer,
a conscript in the tsar's army,
or a heretic massacred in medieval France.
Not history but a fable without a beginning
other than daybreak or an ending other
than a diaspora of stars in the black-velvet sky
as each tree, deciduous and evergreen, fades
into the deepening gloom without protest,
and the water courses its way downstream
as winter melts, the wind gathers and guides
the light on its back like a swarm of bees.

19.

Happy the man who stays awake in the dark
alone with his thoughts as useful as bridges
built to be crossed by armies and blown up
by boys in drab green uniforms whose whole life
took place on a single night in a foxhole
in the coldest December on record and the men
in the platoon knew that only three of the five
would survive the night but which three
nobody knew and so each took turns saying
what he would do for his fallen comrades
if he should be the one favored by fortune
who returns to his native town dearer to him
than the marble of monuments, majesty of courts,
Doric temples in adoration of the golden calf.

20.

What does he believe in? The logic of
a binary opposition: the Greeks and the Hebrews,
the aesthetic and the ethical, sunlight and gloom,
gods made in man's athletic image and god as
the voice that walks in the cool of the evening
casting a blue shadow in the marvelous garden.
The man and the woman are naked and hiding
but who told them they were naked;
did sex come into the world with their sin
or had they mated when innocent?
The story made sense, even the absence
of an underworld, which he invented
in a cave on the far side of the falls
where ghosts loiter and sunlight fails.

21.

What did he believe in? He believed in nothing
and painted it wrote odes to it composed the music
that other poets listen to when writing their odes to nothing.
He believed the conception of divinity as cruel
was probably healthy, though he was too soft-hearted
to live like the gladiators who fought to the death
and merged their bodies with concubines in bed,
the oldest and most primitive form of intoxication.
The fall of water drowned all else but the concept
of the day (dread), the poem of the day ("Ulysses"),
and the moment when a man and a woman know
they will make love for the first time. The hero knows
he shall win at the odds. But thou wouldst not
think how ill all's here about his heart,
that stop-sensation on his soul, and thunder in the room.

22.

What did he believe in? Guilt,
not the remorse that follows lust in action
but the guilt at daybreak on waking
from dreams of killing a friend and
taking his place in the bed of the muse
in her sophomore year at Barnard when
he was happy as the son of Ulysses
seeking news of his father and supping
with the red-haired king and his wife,
the most beautiful and fickle of abducted
queens, who put a potion into her husband's
goblet and her own, and now they can feast
to their hearts' content oblivious
to the suffering and sorrow they caused.

23.

Happy the hero who hears the song
while strapped to the mast in loin-cloth clad,
his muscular chest exposed, the curls
on his forehead glistening in the sweat
of the midday sun, and he knows they are
singing for him, singing of their desire
for him, which he is powerless to prevent
or fulfill, powerless to do anything but speak
the words that will always evoke the sun
and the salt air and the smell of the sea
and the wind from the west that guided
the galleon. Happy as Ulysses
embarking on his last voyage is he,
is nobody, who believes in nothing.

24.

What did he believe in? Lies, all lies.
Happy the man who utters only such lies
as allow him to defeat his enemies
outwit his foes and spirit away the star
of the Mummers and the Footlights.
But decades go by as fast as years
and the boy beloved by the naked goddess
is an old man who hates going to the doctor
hates the pills that let him sleep but rob him
of his appetite, and she who once played
the lead in *A Midsummer Night's Dream*
is waiting for him to wake up and thank her
for teaching him that the brain unchained
is the brilliant body shorn of clothes.

25.

Happy is she whom Ulysses loves more
than the princess who can never grow old
who clothed him in robes, purple and gold,
when the shipwreck brought him to her shore.
Happy is she whom he loves more than
the goddess on the isle heart-sore
with love for him who changes daily, daily grows
more homesick for a past that comes and goes
too fast. Happy as Ulysses landing on the shore
of Ithaca unchanged but in the guise
of a man twenty years older than when he set forth
and now he has come to his own house, armed with lies,
a beggar in rags, preparing to beat
the odds and regain the blissful seat.

26.

Happy as Ulysses is the man who goes forth
as if for the first time though
he has sailed these waters before.
But in poetry it is always the first time,
the first time a man and a woman kiss
after each has joined the other's rhyme:
joy unlimited except, perhaps, for the rules
of monogamy and the appointed roles
of husband and wife before the law
they accept as necessary rituals like
washing the feet of strangers who
visit you in your desert enclave
and only after they leave can you tell
they are angels on the way to harrow hell.

27.

Happy as Penelope is she who doesn't see
the scar on her husband's thigh. Happy
as their son is the boy picked last
who scores the winning goal. Happiest,
the sailor who loved the crone, who said,
"a blind man can recognize his daughter
by touching her face with his fingers,"
and joyous tears follow the long separation.
But Ulysses expects more. He believes
the bed he built in his olive tree will be
where he left it when he left Ithaca to the minstrels
and swineherds and nursemaids who recognize him.
He knows he exists because his dog knows him
and follows him across the stream and into the woods.

28.

Ulysses lived in the age of youth, and if
he crossed the channel in a small fishing skiff,
it was to find a woman to bear his seed,
a maiden bearing a bucket of well water for him
and one for his crew after their hard passage.
He brought her home, then resumed his life
of adventure. Yet there were days of doubt, days he felt
like a European father watching his grown-up son
cheat on his taxes and his wife.
The dad, a man of many wiles, still intent
on getting home, shakes his head in amazement:
Why do you want to hurt me so much?
And the son is America, wondering:
Is this part of the punishment?

29.

At night when he drifted into the darkness,
he heard the laughter of the ghosts and saw them
like cobwebs in the entrance of a cave.
It was then he knew the end was near. Five summers
like five winters in unheated cabins exposed to the wind
and hail frequent in that northern clime. Still, he vowed
to act as if no harm could befall him, and when
there was an adventure to be had, he went.
He didn't withdraw sulking into his tent
like the team's braggart right-fielder but took
his place in the batter's box and hit bad pitches over the wall.
That was then. Now he still had friends though all
they did was die. It was hard to shake off the lethargy.
Well, he deserved a holiday, if only to attend the funeral.

30.

When the end comes where will we be? Will it drizzle,
will it be April, will we drive along the coast and go
back to where we slaughtered the oxen of the sun
and mingled among man-eating monsters; will we go
back to sea one more time in search of caves of
hidden treasure, unforbidden pleasure; will we know
how to answer the doctor with his no-nonsense air when
he comes shining his pocket torch into our pupils to see
if we are compos mentis; will Ulysses still be Ulysses glad
though now his fondest wish is to die in his own bed
after one last adventure abroad, because he can't help himself,
he has to go before the mast, a week of peace and quiet
at home is as much as he can bear
before he journeys to endure the conquest of fear.

II.
Gifts Reserved for Age

Let me disclose the gifts reserved for age
To set a crown upon your lifetime's effort.

—T. S. Eliot, "Little Gidding"

1. "Now that he was here . . ."

Now that he was here, now that he'd arrived,
a survivor on this crowded isle of cannibals
on cannabis texting on their smart phones,
he went to spy school and donned a disguise

to infiltrate the mob with as little compromise
as his career allowed. There were always a few
who stood ready to accuse him of being a Jew
and potential victim. Luckily, he was invisible,

and late for the meeting across the street.
Like a bar without liquor, here he could meet
people from the Bronx he would not otherwise meet.

"I've been sober for ten years. Not a sip of gin,"
though he still confuses pleasure with sin
and death with last year's date on a vial of medicine.

2. Leap of Faith

Philosophy was one of the benefits of age
as was knowing that all protest is futile.
The mind cannot contend with envy and rage,
and yet you feel the anger of a justified sinner.

Even here, in Emerson's land of self-reliance,
the mob is always getting mobilized,
and the show would bring tears to your eyes
or make you shake your head in disbelief

except, well, you're on the roof with some guy
who wants to jump, or wants you to tell him why
he shouldn't jump when every day

is a new torment, and you try to sell him
on America, and a good night's sleep,
but you lose the dispute, and he slips.

3. Dream Audience

Justify the wrath but do not let it show.
It is unworthy of you. When you are handsome,
you convey enthusiasm, joy, the pleasure
of performing before a dream audience
as you get set to relive your life
one night at a time, dying in your bed
at home, before the pills begin to work.
Life, your life, isn't as complicated
as the tax code or the criminal justice system,
but you were lucky enough to have dated
the past when it was still the March night
and you were avid to live it. Relive it
as you write it. The first sentence goes right
to left, the second left to right.

4. The Triumph of Bullshit

They had trained him to throw the first stone
across the border. The moment had come and gone.
He was damned as long as he stayed in this city,
so he got on the train, went to the state university,
majored in philosophy. It didn't matter whether or not
he believed. To affirm something, a fiction even,
was a good way to deal with what T. S. Eliot
called "the triumph of bullshit." Eliot could see it:
God had died but smart people didn't have to believe it
in England in 1940. *You smile, and the angels sing*
is what he heard in the temple that May morning
in what sounded like Martha Tilton's voice,
proving that music can erupt even here,
and the Benny Goodman band took it from there.

5. Doing Philosophy

Philosophy requires us to begin
with a tabula rasa—a clean slate,
which is like giving a clean bill of health
to a chain smoker and functioning alcoholic.

At Berkeley, there's a bishop who believes
nothing exists except his own mind.
Days he lies beneath a tree and studies
the clouds on the ceiling. On this island

of ideas where monstrous bodies married
to the wrong mind or the righteous soul dwell,
the thinker will, from a cemetery by the sea,

contemplate evil as a proof of divinity,
the way religion converts
contradiction into paradox.

6. Think About It

Think about it. You can't
because you can't
even begin because
what does it mean to begin

where do we come from
how do we know what we know
and other insoluble chess problems
played without a board without

chessmen white and black like
Milton Avery's fencers in the picture
we chose for the year's cover,

and the dignity of the foes
with foils in their hands:
unthinkable today.

7. Que sais-je?

The audience splits in two, like boys playing punch ball,
creating two teams, the sophists versus the poets.

The sophists ask: What do I know? The question,
good enough for Montaigne, meant three things:
he wanted to know as much as he could;
he knew he knew nothing; and he knew
no "truth" holds true for any but a few,
all time condensed into a moment fading fast
into the irrecoverable. Mired in the dust
of creation, can we fly? Nor can we breathe
underwater. Yet we, the products of lust,
presume to vault the heavens without fear.

To which the poets respond with a wink, a leer,
a drink, a speech in the storm from mad King Lear.

8. Masks of Woe

The poets undo your invisible mending
with Que Sais-Je, a fragrance from 1925, blending
hazelnut, honey, and peach. Beyond understanding,
it's a license to emulate the wonder
of a butterfly distracting a thinker,
a bee inspecting a rose, a grumble of thunder.

A compelling case can be made for either
the poets or the sophists, so he shirks the task.

Some of the marks of woe he sees are masks
of envy, and envy is almost always an error,
because the envied one has lost a spouse to disease,
or a daughter to a sniper's bullet, or both parents
in a plane crash, or his way in a dark forest,
or some other misfortune graver than one's own.

9. The Trial

He had the same name as someone who fought battles
or hit home runs. "No," he said. "I'm the other one,
but I get a lot of his phone calls." *You smile, and the angels
sing*, and your idea of America amounts to an elegy
for the blue postal box on our street named for a tree,
and the box is gone. Ah, well, you did get to go on the radio
to bewail the latest outrage in Florida or Fresno
or crimes against the humanities at Harvard and Yale.
There were these two attorneys, Bribe and Bail,
and each knew how to foul up your memory.
You owned up to living in the previous century,
recalling the glamour of jazz clubs in January.
God? God had died, but the smart money
continued to keep Him enthroned.

10. Good News

Poems unfinished, the slow decay, the sail
underwater, too heavy to lift, and the empty pail
of fullfed beasts: these were the gifts reserved for age.
He has heard it before. It's time to turn the page.

Therefore, one night he loses something on a bus—
a briefcase, a manuscript, the notes of an address
he can wing. Relieved, he must admit; urban chaos
has been good to him. Life, his life, is less eerie

than mutual assured destruction or modern monetary theory.
It was just as the astrologist advised. Don't worry:
his mother would live to be ninety-four; he would marry

the right woman. And on a day of no news (good news,
unless you run a newspaper), last season's brood
of unhappy kids miss their happy childhood.

11. Breakdown

The plot came to an arguably premature climax
when the car broke down and no one was watching.
There were danger signs all over, but the two of them
couldn't resist. It was summer, unbearably hot,

and the stream was just wide enough to swim in.
So they took off their clothes, left them on a rock,
and swam. Later, dressed, what were they thinking?
It was the closest thing to making love without linking.

That was wonderful, and when the rental car
broke down beside a golden meadow
of haystacks in the midsummer glow,

she told him she loved him, was glad to be lost
with him without a map, and wore
lipstick the color of rouge in film noir.

12. Creation

The red satin was meant for her to wear
with any of the many ways she wore her hair.
If love, the love of his mate, was all that stood
between nothing and oblivion, he knew he should

write love poems to her, sonnets, a century of prose.
The job of the poet was to write poems in praise
of creation, and what work of the Lord could surpass
the creation of Eve, mother of us all, or the three Graces

in the green *primavera*? Was her image
that of Esther, daring to disturb the king, or Aphrodite
frolicking with Ares in the net the cuckold crafted?

Did he sleep with her, and bicker with her after,
ashamed of their bodies when they wake
after fitful sleep, flesh of his flesh, sleep of her sleep?

13. Love and Destiny

There was a time when the worship of a woman
with the intent to couple with her was
the unspoken goal of all well-born men
in love with love, as Plato predicted,
and formed the backbone of literature.
Consider the medieval French romance.
The hero's problem, now that he has arrived,
has mated with a woman, is how to return to
worldly duties, the need to make money
and fight duels? Love and destiny were
not always in alignment. For more than a year
the hero had to win the woman then lose her
then win her a second time before
bidding her adieu in front of her door.

14. September Evening

She couldn't fake the joy in her voice
when he called, or the wild look in her eyes
when she caught sight of his long loping stride
coming toward her on the sidewalk, a whiff
of melons in the air, tobacco smoke and perfume,
September in the city. And he could feel it
coming on, the old rogue feeling, as if
the romance of his life were about to begin
back in his city again. He wore an expectant grin.
What a boy he still was, crossing the street
against the light, sure he could come to no harm,
looking dazed, afraid he was late, when he saw
the look on her face, and knew it was for him.

15. The Only Real Thing

If it's victor versus vanquished, which shall you be?
In England he learned the rites of resignation.
In France he cleansed his palate between courses.
He had to admit he was the hero of his own life
but so was everyone else, so the distinction
was meaningless. Everyone was equal, no one
gave a damn, and just about the only real thing left
was money, the figures in the financial pages
and the exchange of cash in the back seat of a car.
Religion was something that existed like heaven,
out of reach but not out of sight
to the Bedouin in a robe of many colors
sleeping under a black sky and a yellow moon
with the sound of a flute in his ear.

16. Senior Seminar

The questions kept coming. Is pinball as good as poetry?
Are opioids the religion of the battered and beaten?
If God is dead, aren't we all heathens?
To live, must you admit that you, too, are vile?

They didn't solve the problem of evil
because they lived in the wrong century, and the Devil
had yet to make his comeback in the blood-soaked land
of vineyards. The instinctive cruelty of children

played its part, and the quarrels among siblings
sent the hero on a journey across frontiers,
a stranger, a loner in a London crowd, lonely, loud.

He reveled in the knowledge
that nobody knew him. Nobody gave him
a second look. There he felt free.

17. Where He Felt Free

To be conscious that the end of a dream is approaching,
and yet has not absolutely come . . .
—Thomas Hardy

Had anything changed, besides the waning light,
since the day he arrived with only a duffel bag?
He still liked the gloom of amber streetlamps,
no sun all day, the deep chill of night
when all creatures withdraw into their caves
and write on the walls to while away the time.
It is medieval, this gloom, like the ashen walls
of buildings that have weathered long
winters of wind and dust and rain
on cobblestone streets, where you walk
invisible though able to see the ghosts
of girls in nightgowns gliding across
the bridge, and the barebacked boys on bicycles
with their long scarves flying in the wind.

18. Grand Central

He was on his way to make a fortune,
but he had a train to catch.
He bought a newspaper at the train station
so as to look like anyone else,
but no one was fooled.
He would have joined the debate
on tariffs and borders,
but he had a train to catch.
He was prepared to argue
that the degradation of culture was
the worst thing about the 2000s
and could make the argument
in five thousand words,
but he had a train to catch.

19. The Commuter

Old feelings like old habits die hard
and even now when he boards a train
he feels like a commuter trying
to get some reading done when
no seats are left in the quiet car.
The train once meant escape
into luxurious boredom or temptation
of danger with a willing stranger,
and the station still stands in relation to romance
as airports to dread and despair.
Back in the day he played chess with a pocket board.
Had anything changed since he began
to scan the golden grain going backward rather than
capture the queen of a rival on board?

20. May Day

On a Sunday in May, maybe it's better to stay
out of the fray: this became his default position.
There was the charm of giving up all ambition,
because he knew the scent of defeat, *m'aidez*

on May Day, the survivor who owes his life
to the fragment of a raft on a wide river
that goes from one shore to the other to deliver
the bad news concealed in the end of strife.

He surfaces in strangely familiar territory
and wanders the streets of the city
that looks almost nothing like the city

of his boyhood, the subject of a story,
with conspirators linking a coffee shop,
an apothecary, a jeweler, and a head shop.

21. "Criticism is death"

If "criticism is death," a triple ring of flames,
the dancer must answer with a flying leap.
The professor as confessor, admiral of sheep.
And the lovers are happy that no one knows their names.

And what do the words mean
to the condemned man facing his last meal
in prison; if you could get him to say what was real
to him at this moment, what book would he read
if he had one more night to kill? Freed
of one illusion, would he cling to the gospel of Freud?

It didn't matter who broke up with whom.
On a May morning of birds, with only a dog for a friend,
He knew the affair had come to an end.
Maybe he should have stayed in his room.

22. A Red Mercedes

He tried to get off the train
but something always stood in the way.
At one stop a red Mercedes awaited him
with the night's unbeatable first sip
from the cup of conjugal love. It was tempting,
but the sound of children at play
so easily mistaken for spontaneous joy
was not what the conductor
promised the traveler. So he read
the same newspaper and carried the same
umbrella as the train pulled into the station
in a windy city where the cold wet pavement
chills the salesman through heel and sole,
and the best restaurant in town closes at ten.

23. Utopia (No Place)

If there was ever a place
of refuge from war
or politics "by other means,"
it should be in this school
but it isn't, it should be
in this temple but it isn't,
it isn't on the airwaves
or in cyberspace he has
looked in libraries and palaces
and he can find it no place,
no place to take the place of home,
the home that Homer saw
in his dreams, the rustic home
the Trojan fled to go to unholy Rome.

24. A Working Heaven

It was easier to write about people
suffering, or fighting, or enduring bad marriages,
than to conceive of a working heaven.

What made it so hard to summon
an earthly paradise, even a false one,
when hell is so vivid a place, a liquor store
robbed, the jagged necks of broken bottles on the floor?

The *Inferno* beats the *Paradiso* hollow.

Maybe paradise was July in Provence with olive trees,
yellow broom, the scents of Grasse, the café of outcasts
who live in caves writing books no one need ever read.

At seven, bottles of Beaujolais appear, and someone
has money enough to foot the bill. —On the train,
he slept past his station once again.

25. Lazy Days

He disagreed with everyone, and didn't want to argue
about it. Beyond this fiddle were things he valued:
the wild look in his lady's eyes when "with kisses four"
he shut them; Keats; the door that led to another door;

the nudity on the rocks near the waterfall;
lazy days for *les idées*; sons and daughters; the tall
palm trees blessing the ballpark in Chavez Ravine;
the day they first coupled; a scoop at the crime scene.

These things were important because the memory
of loss was as constant as the loss of memory, and
the whole of his ambition was to lie unclothed in the sun.

Let it be that August day, let the clouds surrender to the sun,
a bath, a shave, maybe a joint, so when he revives,
he feels equal to the nervousness of being alive.

26. The Eternal Moment

Shame he seldom felt, but glory remained
like dust on the spines of books on the shelves.
He wondered which of his several selves
he should leave in the room like a vial of pills
or a wristwatch engraved with her initials.
But it was raining and he had to catch a train
to a place that still seemed as distant as the pain
he left behind when he married the muse
of his eternal moment. She departed
without valediction as the train
left the phantom station, and what remained
amid the whistles and shouts, and taxis in the rain,
was the sadness of art crafted by the downhearted
who discovered their shadows on the train.

27. Lessons Learned

Anyone can be bought, anyone can be sold,
anyone can be called, anyone can be rolled.
For every angry minute you lose
sixty seconds of happiness. Ceaseless
as the cricket, all night till dawn flow her tears.
A strong prison requires no bars.
You can't think well unless you've dined well.
You can't keep a secret unless you hide it from yourself.
Nevertheless, there is pleasure in the pathless woods where
you can bray all night before you shake down the stars.
Love, built of beauty, dies when beauty dies.
There are two tragedies in life,
and whatever they are, you will endure them,
like a heart that breaks but continues to beat.

28. History

History is (a) a restaurant with too many
menu options (b) a textbook (c) an unsolved
murder (d) repetitive, atonal, abstract,
and as foreign to the mind of the future

as the printed word is fated to be. Oh, there will be
antique stores, museums, minor monuments,
the fittest books surviving in deckle-edged paper,
and maybe Shakespeare will lead the pack

once scholars acknowledge he was a woman.
You plan in the past, you stumble in the present,
you fail in the future, and you call that history.

History is loss, is dictated by the boss. History is
a waste of time, but it's also a string of syllables,
the train schedule, the maze, the garden, the hills.

29. The Pious Donors

The people are the same, as are the passions,
only the décor has changed, the fashions,
and though you wouldn't guess it,
the donors depicted in the blessed
triptych of a golden annunciation may be
scoundrels as vicious as any since. History
is an attic visited by an agnostic insomniac. But life,
your life, isn't as complicated as the stages of grief,
a public assassination, a crisis in belief.
Without knowing why, our hero remains a do-or-die
agent betrayed by his boss. He doubts everything but clings
to the ignorance that is the mother of all things,
even extraterrestrial forces or the fury of the sea,
the violated earth, the unforgiving sky.

30. "Not that he was here . . ."

Not that he was here, not that he'd arrived,
but that the questions would never cease
and the well-thumbed books remain on their shelves—
that was his tentative conclusion.
Will the poor always be with us? Do all pronouns
refer to one dreamer, a stranger, a loner
in a throng of strangers? Where was he going?
Was there time enough for one more trip?
But the train made an unscheduled stop, and he got out,
and walked away from protesters and police
and the customary crowd of spectators.
Was it for this that he gave up the god
of the fathers? Would he stumble on the right answer
now that he was here, now that he'd arrived?

Previous Winners of the New Criterion Poetry Prize

Christopher Hewitt, *The Summer After*
Peter Vertacnik, *The Nature of Things Fragile*
Brian Brodeur, *Some Problems with Autobiography*
Nicholas Pierce, *In Transit*
Bruce Bond, *Behemoth*
Ned Balbo, *The Cylburn Touch-Me-Nots*
Nicholas Friedman, *Petty Theft*
Moira Egan, *Synæsthesium*
John Foy, *Night Vision*
Michael Spence, *Umbilical*
John Poch, *Fix Quiet*
Dick Allen, *This Shadowy Place*
George Green, *Lord Byron's Foot*
D. H. Tracy, *Janet's Cottage*
Ashley Anna McHugh, *Into These Knots*
William Virgil Davis, *Landscape and Journey*
Daniel Brown, *Taking the Occasion*
J. Allyn Rosser, *Foiled Again*
Bill Coyle, *The God of This World to His Prophet*
Geoffrey Brock, *Weighing Light*
Deborah Warren, *Zero Meridian*
Charles Tomlinson, *Skywriting and Other Poems*
Adam Kirsch, *The Thousand Wells*
Donald Petersen, *Early and Late: Selected Poems*